Katie Piper

Start Your Day
With Katie

I dedicate this book to my loving parents, David and Diane. Thank you for filling my head with positive thoughts every day and ensuring our house was filled with an abundance of love and good energy.

I love you. x

Katie Piper

Start Your Day
With Katie

365 Affirmations for a Year
of Positive Thinking

Quercus

First published in Great Britain in 2012 by
Quercus
55 Baker Street
7th Floor, South Block
London
W1U 8EW

A CIP catalogue record for this book is available
from the British Library.

ISBN 978 1 78087 659 7

2 4 6 8 10 9 7 5 3 1

Cover photograph © Ray Burmiston / www.shootgroup.com
Hand lettering: www.ruthrowland.co.uk
Text designed and typeset by Bob Vickers

Printed and bound in Portugal

INTRODUCTION

For those of you who know about my road to recovery after the acid attack that disfigured my face, you'll know that positive affirmations were hugely helpful to me in my search for strength. They helped me turn my negative thoughts around so that I could move forward with my life, and they really, really worked. I continue to use them every day, whether or not I'm going through a tough time. Now I want to share them with you!

This book is a collection of positive thoughts, mantras and inspirational quotes that I find incredibly uplifting and thought-provoking. Some focus on goals – such as health or happiness; others are a reminder that no matter what we're going through, we are not alone. If you can approach all of your life – the good *and* the bad – with a positive outlook, you are more likely to come out the other side with a smile on your face. As I've said before: if you believe, you will survive.

In this book you'll find an entry for each day of the year, but of course you can read them in any order, and once you've found the ones that speak loudest to you, you can use them again and again. Why not try writing down your favourite entries and putting them around your house to give you a boost whenever you walk past? I've added my own thoughts to some of my favourite affirmations and important dates, explaining why they hold particular significance to me.

At the start of each month you'll also find a 'monthly mantra' – phrases that reinforce a loving attitude towards yourself. I find that saying these mantras out loud makes them even more powerful, so try memorizing and repeating them to your-self whenever you need comfort, reassurance or encouragement.

I hope this book will help you find peace, happiness and inspiration whenever you need it!

JANUARY

JANUARY

1

Monthly Mantra

'From today I will think about the
good things to come in my life, and let go
of things that may have happened in the past.
I can make great things happen!'

As this is the start of your new year, use this month to think about new
beginnings! This is your mantra for January: say it out loud to yourself
every day as a reminder to stay positive and keep looking forward!
You can even write it down and tape it to your bathroom mirror
so that you see it first thing every morning and last thing
before you go to sleep.

Life is 10 per cent what happens to you
and 90 per cent how you react to it.

Positive change can begin
whenever you want it to;
just be willing to embrace it
when it comes.

JANUARY

4

To reach a goal you must know
what it is you want to achieve and believe
in yourself that you can get there.

JANUARY

5

Today is a new day, a new start –
no matter what happened yesterday.

'It is never too late
to be what you might have been.'
George Eliot

Our lives are full of opportunities
waiting to be seized.

Treat your mind with the same respect
you treat your body. Consider unhealthy
thoughts the same way you do unhealthy food.
Set limits and focus on what will nourish you.

Try something new every day,
and every day your world will get
bigger and bigger.

JANUARY
10

Life doesn't come
with an instruction booklet,
so write your own!

'Be not afraid of going slowly,
be afraid only of standing still.'
Chinese proverb

Stop preparing and
start doing!

Live every day with love,
not fear.

You have an inner strength
that might surprise you; once you've
discovered it you will always know
that you can turn to it to achieve anything.

JANUARY
15

Today is the day that you
can choose to make a difference,
to your life or to somebody else's.
Do something wonderful!

'Nothing in life is to be feared.

It is only to be understood.'

Marie Curie

The people who love you most will
give you the freedom to be what you want.
Show others that same love.

Another person's actions may cause you
pain but they do not determine your future;
have confidence and know that you
are in control of your choices in life,
whatever comes your way.

Regardless of whether you succeed
or fail, what's important is that you
tried in the first place.

JANUARY
20

Accept the things you cannot change
and make positive changes to the things
you can. You'll find you have the power
to change more than you expect.

'Don't judge each day by the harvest
you reap, but by the seeds you plant.'
Robert Louis Stevenson

When something stops you in your tracks,
think: is this a problem or an opportunity?
Once you've identified it, you can
make it work for you.

At the beginning of my recovery, I often felt like my scars weren't
healing quickly enough and every time I had a setback I found it really
demoralizing. But eventually I learned to look at challenges or obstacles
as an opportunity to prove how strong and motivated I could be.
When you're forced to take a different direction in life, it can
sometimes lead to things you never even expected!

We have many tools within us.
For every challenge, we just need to identify
the necessary tool and learn how best to use it
to make our life a masterpiece.

Focus on the good things in life, no matter
how small, and they will multiply.

All life experiences are connected,
the pieces of the jigsaw you put in place today
will be part of who you are in the future.

'There are two ways of spreading light:
to be the candle or the mirror that reflects it.'
Edith Wharton

Weather the storms in your life,
for calm will inevitably follow.

Believe that you are moving
in the right direction. Follow your feet
and trust that you are choosing
the best path.

If your life seems full of darkness,
look and see if it is you who is
blocking the light.

A bad judgement should not stop you in your tracks; it is merely an obstacle on the path to your goal. Step around it and keep going forward.

Bravery is daring to try
where others would not.

FEBRUARY

1

Monthly Mantra

'I am loved and supported and I don't have to go through life on my own. I can ask for help and comfort when I need it, and will give it back to others when they need it in return.'

February is the month of love, both giving and receiving, so what better time to remind yourself that people love you and want the best for you, whether it's your partner, family or friends.

FEBRUARY

2

Look in the mirror every day and
remind yourself what you want from life.
Say it out loud, like you mean it and want it,
and send it into the universe, from where
it can't be taken back.

'Go confidently in the direction of your dreams. Live the life you've imagined.'

Henry David Thoreau

FEBRUARY

4

Everything happens for a reason,
but we don't always need to know
what that reason is. Enjoy the surprises
as your life unfolds.

Accept your imperfections; as you grow
and move through the stages of your life
be aware that what bothers you now will not
necessarily bother you in the future.

It's easiest to find happiness when
you know what will make you happy.
Realize this, and happiness is yours
for the taking.

'No bird soars too high if he soars
on his own wings.'
William Blake

Open your heart to trust today;
an open heart will draw others
towards you.

FEBRUARY

9

Smiles can make even the darkest day
look brighter. Be generous with them!

10

Life is not measured by the number
of breaths we take, but by the moments
that take our breath away.

Nobody ever climbed a mountain
by saying, 'I can't.'

Silence is a great healer. Let yourself
block out the noise of the world from time to
time and listen to your inner voice –
it will tell you what you need.

'Far away there in the sunshine are my highest aspirations. I may not reach them, but I can look up and see their beauty, believe in them, and try to follow where they lead.'

Louisa May Alcott

FEBRUARY

14

Meet life with love and you will
find love in life.

I really believe this. When you love yourself and take care of yourself,
other people will be attracted to your confidence. But remember that
you don't need another person to be complete, even on Valentine's!
I often buy myself flowers – just to treat myself.

FEBRUARY
15

You are who you are. Love yourself,
cherish your qualities and marvel at your
uniqueness. The more you love and respect
yourself, the more others will love
and respect you.

If you feel scared about what's ahead,
look to others who got there before you.

Life is never predictable. If you accept
that life will be full of surprises you will
be more prepared to deal with whatever
comes your way.

Let others help guide you,
but don't let them control you.

At those times when your life feels out of
control, tell yourself: 'I control my choices,
and the choices I make will decide my future!'
Then make the best choices you can!

'No kind action ever stops with itself.
The greatest work that kindness does to others
is that it makes them kind themselves.'

Amelia Earhart

Though you may have been hurt in love,
it does not mean you are unlovable.
Keep your heart open to being loved again,
as if it was the first time.

If you want to change your world,
first you have to change your ways.

If you can see potential in every opportunity,
you will feel the rewards that each
opportunity brings.

Embrace the challenges that today brings –
they will only make you stronger.

'What does not kill me makes me stronger.'

J. W. Goethe

Forgiveness can help you find inner peace –
if you start to forgive yourself or others today,
the peace in your heart will follow.

Accept compliments whenever they are given
– you deserve them!

Every day is a brand new day:
put yesterday behind you, deal with
tomorrow when it comes, and let today
be positive and productive.

MARCH

Monthly Mantra

'I am important and will take good care
of my mind, my body and my soul. If I look
after myself as I should, I will open the door
to a healthy, happy life.'

March is a time to celebrate mothers and those who look after us –
whether it's your mum, another relative, a friend or even a supportive
teacher – so take a lesson from those people and let this month's
mantra remind you to give yourself all that nurturing support, too.
For me, March has also become a month of strength, as it's when my
attacks took place. Celebrate your strength on the 8th,
which is International Women's Day.

'Life appears to me too short to be spent in nursing animosity, or registering wrongs.'

Charlotte Brontë

We are more than how we look,
and more than the things that we own.
Our souls are beautiful, and we all have
a part to play in this exciting world.

MARCH
4

Be open to new ideas, new possibilities and new directions – see the world as an amazing place and it will leave you wide-eyed with wonder.

Aim high in whatever you do;
it doesn't matter how long it takes to get there,
just know that every step you take is
upwards towards your goal.

'I have made it a rule of my life never to regret and never to look back. Regret is an appalling waste of energy . . . you can't build on it; it's only good for wallowing in.'

Katherine Mansfield

Have faith that you will experience joy
and contentment today and every day.

Aim for progress, not perfection.
Nobody's perfect, so don't put pressure on
yourself to achieve the impossible. Enjoy who
you are with all your imperfections!

There is more than one way forward in life;
if you have trouble on one path,
try creating a new one.

Open your eyes to the loving people around you: see their special qualities and cherish the relationships that mean so much to you. They will be your rocks in life whatever comes your way.

'Life is ours to be spent,

not to be saved.'

D. H. Lawrence

Step back from your problems for today
and make the effort to help someone else.
You will see how it lifts their spirit –
and your own.

If you choose not to try, you are defeated
before you begin; you can only succeed
if you choose to try.

MARCH

14

Your emotions are like an onion;
there are lots of tiny layers and only when you
have peeled each one away can you get
to what is going on inside.

Your current blessings are far more
powerful than your past regrets.

'We must walk consciously only part way
toward our goal and then leap in the dark
to our success.'
Henry David Thoreau

MARCH
17

Speak about what you can and will do,
not about what you can't and won't.

The more you believe in yourself, the more others will put their belief in you, too.

If you open your eyes and heart to the love
around you, it can only lift your spirits.

For every fear there is hope; for every worry
there is peace – remember to see both sides
and find balance and harmony in your life.

'Act as though what you do
makes a difference. It does.'
William James

Whatever you do, give it your all.
Throw yourself in with confidence,
and throw doubts and fears aside.

What we think and what we say
are just as important as what we do.

Treat others with kindness and trust
that your kindnesses will be repaid.

MARCH
25

Exercise your right to have the life you want;
if you decide not to make choices you risk
that the choices will be made for you.

Laughter breeds more laughter,
so seek out those things that delight you
and feel them lift your soul.

The price of wisdom is often pain,
but all experience teaches us something –
if we choose to learn from it.

This is the date of my first attack in 2008, but I've refused to let it
become a day of negative memories. I've worked really hard to
reclaim it – this affirmation reminds me that I survived and helps me
to focus on everything I've learned and all the positive things
that have happened since.

'Fear is only as deep as the mind allows.'

Japanese proverb

With every challenge comes fulfilment;
with every disappointment comes strength.

What happened in the past is done with –
it is the actions you take next that will
shape the rest of your life.

MARCH

31

The pain you may feel today will become
the strength you find tomorrow.

Those who know my story might know that this is the date when I had
acid thrown at me. This affirmation resonates with me so much:
I went through terrible, terrible pain back then, but eventually
I managed to pick myself up and it taught me that I'm
stronger than I ever realized.

APRIL

APRIL

1

Monthly Mantra

'I will push myself to try something new every day, even if it seems scary or difficult. I can do anything I put my mind to.'

Spring is such a wonderful time when we're surrounded by new life everywhere we look. Your own growth is important, too, so this month's mantra will help you sow the seeds to expand your horizons and step out of your comfort zone.

Even if you can't find a reason to smile,
do it anyway!

Let others see in you the things
you love most about yourself.

'I am not discouraged, because every wrong
attempt discarded is another step forward.'
Thomas Edison

Creativity nourishes the soul:
get creative, do the things you love
and feel the pleasure that it brings.

Failures are milestones on the road to achievement. It is when you look back that you can see how far you've come.

Celebrate every victory over fear
and feel the courage it gives you
for the next challenge.

It doesn't matter where you find faith;
just believe and feel the strength it gives you.

For me, faith was believing that things could get better,
and not giving up. I found my faith in God, but you can reach out
to anything that helps you stay strong and hopeful.

'The best way to cheer yourself is to try to cheer somebody else up.'

Mark Twain

APRIL

10

If you feel anger, acknowledge it,
then learn to let it go. The more it lingers,
the greater it grows.

Be kind to yourself – aim to do your best,
do not aim for perfection.

It only takes one person to help you
find happiness in life, and that's you!

APRIL

13

Take the time to stop and appreciate
the beauty in nature – it will remind you
that there is so much to enjoy in this world
that doesn't cost a thing.

'If you have built castles in the air, your work
need not be lost; that is where they should be.
Now put the foundations under them.'
Henry David Thoreau

What's right for you today
may not be right for you tomorrow,
give yourself permission to grow and to
change your mind, and learn from
your new wisdom.

The best inventions are made by people
who are told, 'You can't', and who
choose not to listen.

'Do not go where the path may lead,
go instead where there is no path
and leave a trail.'

Ralph Waldo Emerson

Life is simpler than you think –
take the time today to enjoy something
simple but wonderful in your life
that normally goes unnoticed.

Be bold with your goals; if you remain
in familiar territory you will never experience
the thrill of the unknown.

'Be not afraid of life. Believe that life
is worth living, and your belief
will help create the fact.'

Henry James

Whatever is happening in your life,
help is only as far as asking for it.

Laughter can offer a perspective
on difficult situations, and let you see
that things are often not as bad
as they may seem.

You're your own teacher and well
of wisdom: listen to everyone's advice but
always remember to listen to your heart.

Seek harmony in your soul
and kindness in the people close to you;
happiness found in material things will not
bring you lasting joy.

'When the student is ready,
the teacher appears.'

Buddhist proverb

Listen to your inner voice – it will be your
closest friend in difficult times and will help
you make good decisions in your life.

Even unremarkable tasks can transform
into pleasures if you learn to recognize that a
positive attitude will carry you through life.

Struggles are a part of our lives;
they enrich our characters, strengthen our
souls and give us the opportunity
to try another way.

'Fairy tales are more than true.

Not because they tell us that dragons exist,

but because they tell us that dragons

can be defeated.'

G. K. Chesterton

Life is full of endings, but every ending
is also a new beginning.

MAY

MAY
1

Monthly Mantra

'I will see the positive side of everything that happens to me. I will see each ending as a new beginning, and each challenge as an opportunity to show how capable I am.'

With flowers in bloom and the days getting longer, May is one of the most optimistic times of the year. Repeat this mantra to help you feel hopeful every day!

If yesterday didn't go the way you planned,
try again today.

Dare to live the life you dream of
and watch your dreams come true.

Focus on the individual steps you need
to take to achieve your goals, rather than
worrying about the entire journey.

'A single act of kindness throws out roots
in all directions, and the roots spring up
and make new trees.'

Amelia Earhart

Fear is an invisible prison; if it controls you, you'll never feel freedom.

The journey through life meets dangers
as well as rewards; greet them both with
courage and strength.

Let your hopes and dreams inspire you
to reach for greater things.

'The foolish man seeks happiness
in the distance, the wise grows it
under his feet.'
James Oppenheim

If you learn to forgive and let go of the past,
you can find release from your anger, pain
and fears, and focus instead on love,
happiness and courage.

I had to let go of a lot of anger towards my attackers. They changed my
life completely, so it would have been easy for me to be consumed with
grief and resentment forever. But while I was letting anger control me,
I wasn't able to actually enjoy life. Once I let go of the anger and moved
on, I was able to make space in my mind for positive feelings again and
suddenly I felt free and hopeful about the future.

If at first you don't succeed – join the club!
We can't all be perfect all the time. The success
lies most in the trying, even if it takes a while
to get the result you want. Don't give up!

Accept people as they are, just as you hope
to be accepted. Those who presume to judge
or change others do so because they
cannot change themselves.

'What we are today comes from our
thoughts of yesterday, and our present
thoughts build our life of tomorrow:
our life is the creation of our mind.'

Buddha

When you feel self-pity pulling you down,
helping others in need will give you
some perspective.

MAY

15

It is better to act than to react.

A positive attitude will open many doors.

'How very little can be done
under the spirit of fear.'
Florence Nightingale

Just because something is right
for someone else, it doesn't mean
it has to be right for you.

Live every moment;
make each one really count.

A book is written word by word,

a house is built brick by brick,

and so your life must take shape

little by little.

MAY

21

'When a person is down in the world,
an ounce of help is better than
a pound of preaching.'
Edward Bulwer-Lytton

MAY

22

How you view the world will determine what you find; if you look for positivity, you will not be disappointed.

When something frustrates or upsets you,
turn the feelings upside-down! Let it motivate
you to make a change in your life.

Love should be unconditional; when you give it in this way you will receive it back in abundance.

'Patience and perseverance have a magical
effect before which difficulties disappear
and obstacles vanish.'
John Quincy Adams

Remind yourself every day that you
are mentally strong, physically strong and
spiritually strong. You have the strength and
power to make every choice a good one.

Only you are the expert on your life,
so pay close attention to your thoughts and
feelings and focus on the ones that you
know are right for you.

Allow yourself to bend like a willow
in the wind, so that you will not break.

Life is full of unexpected opportunities,
so look around you and seize them
whenever they arise.

'Pain is inevitable; suffering is optional.'

Hindu saying

If your opinions of yesterday
and the ideals you once held no longer fit
into your life, put them aside and choose a
new attitude for the new day.

JUNE

JUNE

1

Monthly Mantra

'I am a strong person and nothing can hurt me.
I can handle whatever problems life throws at
me and will bounce back up and carry on.'

June is a time to recognize our fathers and kind male role models –
those who have given us strength, protection and motivation.
Repeat this mantra every day to help you feel the courage
to face up to life's challenges.

Give your best every day, for we have
the power to make the world
as good as we want.

Asking for help is a sign of strength;
it takes courage to admit you can't solve
everything on your own.

'The really great make you feel that you,
too, can become great.'
Mark Twain

Fear is as much of your own making
as is your success. Make your choice wisely.

However long or short the road ahead,
take little steps and eventually you will
reach your destination.

This is an important lesson I learned from my surgeon, Mr Jawad.
He helped me realize that my recovery couldn't happen all at once
and showed me how to break it down into manageable steps, instead of
feeling overwhelmed. It meant that every day I had an achievement to
celebrate, however small!

JUNE

7

The unknown can be scary, but if you face
it with courage and faith in what the future
holds, you'll find your fears slip away.

JUNE

8

When you let go of pride,
you let humility and compassion in.
They will open up your world and allow you
to see the richness of life.

'Beauty is not caused. It is.'

Emily Dickinson

Happiness can be found if you stop to
appreciate all the things you've achieved,
no matter how small.

JUNE

11

Sometimes the greatest opportunities
come at the unlikeliest of times. Keep your
mind and heart open and you'll always be
ready to seize them.

Remember that everyone has troubling times;
when you are feeling down, reach out to others
– whether you help them or they help you,
together you will be stronger.

'Start by doing what's necessary,
then do what's possible, and suddenly
you are doing the impossible.'
St Francis of Assisi

Forgiveness lets you enjoy today without feeling hung up on yesterday.

When you clear the negative thoughts
out of your head, you create space for positive
actions and emotions.

You have the power to be your own
best friend. Stand tall even when you have
made a mistake, help yourself up and give
yourself encouragement to try again.

Love the life you have,

not the one you think you should have.

Make it your own.

'What you get by achieving your goals
is not as important as what you become
by achieving your goals.'

J. W. Goethe

You are not alone on your journey
through life – walk with others and find the
joy and support in shared experiences.

Face each new day with the best of
intentions. Be bold, aim high and be
positive in all that you do.

'I am no bird; and no net ensnares me;
I am a free human being with an
independent will.'
Charlotte Brontë

22

Be generous with your love and you will
feel it returned tenfold.

The people around you can help you make
your choices in life, but the final decision
must always be yours.

Your greatest achievement
is not in the success, but in overcoming
the obstacles along the way.

Be open to new solutions;

they may just solve your old problems.

'As you go the way of life
you will see a great chasm. Jump.
It is not as wide as you think.'
Native American proverb

Cherish the gifts that each day brings
and be grateful they came your way.

People can only hurt you on the inside
if you allow them to. Rise above the bad things
others may have done to you and learn
to put them behind you.

Every tiny positive change you make
in your life offers a nugget of hope
for the future.

Grey skies don't have to mean rain.

It's always sunny above the clouds.

JULY

JULY
1

Monthly Mantra

'The world is a wonderful place
and I am lucky to be a part of it!'

This month, give yourself the room to step back from your stresses
or challenges, even if just for a few moments, and simply let yourself
feel happy! Repeat this mantra each day and smile! No matter what is
happening in your life, remember you are allowed to feel joy.

'What lies behind us and what lies before us
are tiny matters compared to what lies within.'
Ralph Waldo Emerson

Celebrate your successes, no matter how small,
and you will find your confidence grows.
Focus on all your positives!

Embrace compromise, not conflict.
If you learn to bend, you may find that
others meet you halfway.

If you can't see the way to reach
the end of the road, start walking
and let your instincts guide you.

Fear of the unknown is an unfounded fear;
save your caution for where it's really needed.

See your setbacks as opportunities, not problems; if you approach them with positivity, they will teach you that you're stronger than you realize.

JULY

8

'Happiness never decreases
by being shared.'
Buddha

All things become easier
when we know we are not alone.

Your problems will not be solved
by complaining, but by doing something
to solve them.

Open doors; don't wait for them to open.
Climb over obstacles; don't wait
for them to move.

Why rush forward to the future
when there is so much to appreciate today?
Stop, look around you and decide that today
you will see only those things that are positive
in your life. The bad can wait for another day.

'Our aspirations are our possibilities.'

Robert Browning

To wish you were someone else
is to waste the person that you are.

We all make mistakes; learn from them
and you can make your life a happier one.

JULY
16

When you are standing at a crossroads,
your instincts can show you the way.
Give credit to your gut feelings
and listen to them.

JULY

17

There is only one life you can truly influence,
and that is yours.

'Vision is the art of seeing the invisible.'

Jonathan Swift

Instead of thinking, 'Why?',
start thinking, 'Why not?!'

Grace and beauty aren't worn on the outside
like clothes or fashion; they are inside you
and will never go out of style.

Once you have found love for yourself,
love from others will follow.

When you accept responsibility for your
choices in life, you will find your power within
and will realize how much control you have
over your happiness.

We shouldn't expect other people to solve all our problems for us. In my
recovery, my doctors and parents were only able to carry me so far – it
wasn't until I took responsibility for my own recovery that I suddenly
started to make significant progress. Unless we're willing to make an
effort, we can't expect success to land at our feet.

JULY

23

Admitting you do not know everything

shows more wisdom than believing

you have all the answers.

'Circumstances do not make the man;
they merely reveal him to himself.'

Epictetus

If things in your life are tasting bitter,
eat something else!

A life without problems offers no
opportunities to show how strong you are.

JULY

27

Life can be as fulfilling and happy
as you are prepared to make it. Get out there
and make it wonderful.

The attitude of a lifetime is not easy
to change overnight; but if you wear
your new outlook every day, it will soon
become your second skin.

'To be what we are, and to become
what we are capable of becoming,
is the only end in life.'
Robert Louis Stevenson

One small positive action today
can make a big difference to your future.

Instead of standing on the sidelines in sorrow, join in and experience the excitement of the game.

AUGUST

AUGUST

1

Monthly Mantra

'I am a kind and loving person
and will let others see my inner beauty.
The way I live my life is much more
important than the way I look.'

Your beauty comes from deep within you, and nobody
can ever take that away. Let this month's mantra remind
you that it's what's on the inside that counts.
Show the world your beautiful self!

Let your mirror reflect your inner beauty.
It's what you feel that counts, not how
you look to others.

'Arrange whatever pieces come your way.'

Virginia Woolf

Help others to help you. Allow them
to show you their love and support.
You need not be alone in your troubles.

If you don't make a start,
you will never reach the finish!

Fear the worst and you will find it,
believe in the best and it will find you.

'Do not spoil what you have by desiring
what you have not; but remember that
what you now have was once among
the things only hoped for.'

Epicurus

Step up to each day with expectation and joy;
it is an unmapped day full of possibilities.

The greatest successes are achieved
in the face of the greatest adversity.

If someone tries to get in the way of your
dreams, find another way around!
Trust yourself and look instead for the people
who are cheering you on.

The more you can bounce back up from disappointment, the sweeter your success will taste.

12

'Cheerfulness, it would appear, is a matter which depends fully as much on the state of things within, as on the state of things without and around us.'

Charlotte Brontë

Remind yourself of the things
that have gone right, instead of dwelling
on what has gone wrong.

When you strive for your goals,
do it for yourself, not to make others happy.
Tell yourself: 'I will be the best I can be,
for me.'

There are many voices inside our heads.
The positive ones will tell you that you are
special and that you can succeed – those are
the only voices worth listening to.

You may feel hurt,
but you are not broken.

'Happiness depends upon ourselves.'

Aristotle

AUGUST

18

When you act as if you can do something,
soon enough you will discover that you can.

I'm a firm believer in this technique. If you pretend hard enough
about something, eventually you can make it become reality.
For example, if you want to be more confident, just hold your head
high and fake it. If you do it enough times, it will start to stick and
become part of who you are!

Your life is not defined by the things
that happen to you, but by the actions
you take in response to them.

AUGUST

20

Let go of worries about things
you can't control; you can only be responsible
for your own behaviour. When you do your
best, you never lose.

Get to know your limitations,
so that you can learn to find a way to work
around and get past them. There is always a
creative way forward.

There is light in every situation;
open your eyes and let it pull you out
of even the darkest places.

'Plan for the future, because that is where you
are going to spend the rest of your life.'

Mark Twain

Be yourself, not the person
others think you should be.
Have confidence in just being you.

If you believe it,

you can become it!

Face today with enthusiasm and joy.
Today will be a good day, and tomorrow
will be even better.

AUGUST

27

'Life is not easy for any of us.
But what of that? We must have perseverance
and above all confidence in ourselves. We must
believe that we are gifted for something and
that this thing must be attained.'

Marie Curie

Share the kindness that's in your soul.
Even the smallest acts of generosity can bring
great joy to yourself and others.

If you approach all you do with love,
you will find love in all that you do.

Accept that things won't always go exactly how you want them to, but learn to recognize what is working in your life, and you will see a way around and beyond your difficulties.

'There are those who give with joy
and that joy is their reward.'
Kahlil Gibran

SEPTEMBER

SEPTEMBER

1

Monthly Mantra

'I need only take one step at a time.
My goals are within reach and every step
brings me closer to achieving them.'

Autumn is a time of transition and a great time of year to set yourself
new goals, whether you're going back to school or university, thinking
about work, or learning new skills. Focus on what you want to
achieve and let this mantra inspire you to get there!

SEPTEMBER

2

The limit on your happiness
is set only by you.

You cannot predetermine your future;
but the choices you make today will help
to shape it, so make them carefully and
you'll reap the rewards.

Save your regrets for the things
you haven't done, rather than for
the things you have done.

The sky is not the limit:

there's a whole universe beyond it!

'The greatest thing in this world
is not so much where we stand as in
what direction we are moving.'

J. W. Goethe

No problem is too small
to be shared.

During troubled times, open up your eyes.
Sometimes in life we begin to see positive
things we've never noticed before.
However bad you feel, never stop searching
for good things all around you.

Today and every day, do one small thing
that makes you happy, and your happiness
will grow every day.

Whatever change today brings,
embrace it, knowing that it is a step forward
into a new adventure.

SEPTEMBER
11

'I am not afraid . . .
I was born to do this.'

Joan of Arc

You deserve respect from yourself
just as much as you deserve
the respect of others.

We are all students and we are all teachers.
If we open our minds, and share our
experience and knowledge generously
with others, our lives will be richer for it.

Let love in and give it back,
and you will feel its healing power.

'Old habits can't be thrown out the upstairs window. They have to be coaxed down the stairs one step at a time.'

Mark Twain

Set yourself free from your past and
you will clear the way for a new future.

If your cup is half empty,
take it to the tap yourself!

Believing you can do something
is the first step to achieving it.

If you can recognize when you are part of a problem, it will help you figure out how you can also be part of the solution.

Let the steps you take today
be the footprints that others follow.

SEPTEMBER

21

'I attribute my success to this –
I never gave or took any excuse.'

Florence Nightingale

SEPTEMBER

22

It is only when you put aside your fears
and limitations that you can discover
the true extent of your abilities.

Look kindly on your scars; let them remind
you that the pain is over, that your wounds
have healed and you are no longer hurting.

I see my scars in the mirror every day, but I have learned to look on
them positively – they remind me that I survived! They show me that I
got through the bad times, healed myself and came out the other side.
Whether your scars are on the outside or on the inside, if you can
learn to look on them kindly it will fill you with optimism
when you see how far you've come.

Bless with love everything and everyone
that you value in your life and open your eyes
to all the amazing things about this wonderful
planet that you live on.

Silence divides us; sharing our experience
brings us together.

SEPTEMBER

26

'I've learned from experience that
the greater part of our happiness or misery
depends on our dispositions and not
on our circumstances.'

Martha Washington

Imagine your life is a book and write
your own story, then live by your words.

When you believe in yourself
you can achieve the unexpected.

Some people grin and bear it.

Others smile and do it.

When you think there is nowhere to go but down, look up and you'll see another way.

OCTOBER

OCTOBER

1

Monthly Mantra

'Fear does not control me. I will take action even when I feel afraid, and will live my life with courage and confidence.'

You have the power within you to confront all your fears and worries, so let Halloween ghouls be the only scary thing you encounter this month! October's mantra will inspire you to face your fears and will help you find the strength to overcome them.

OCTOBER

2

A smile cures more than
any medicine.

OCTOBER

3

'It is not the failure of others
to appreciate your abilities that should
trouble you, but rather your failure to
appreciate theirs.'

Confucius

OCTOBER

4

To know that you have survived before
is to know that you will do so again.

I often remind myself of this during difficult times. I hope that nothing in my life will be as hard as recovering from my attacks, but I know that if I could get through something as horrendous as that, then I can get through anything! Think back to moments in your own life when you overcame something difficult – remember how you coped and let it give you confidence that you can do the same again.

We have no power over the events
of each new day, but we do have power
over our attitude towards them.

'There will be rubs and disappointments
everywhere, and we are all apt to expect too
much; but then, if one scheme of happiness
fails, human nature turns to another;
if the first calculation is wrong, we make a
second better: we find comfort somewhere.'

Jane Austen

You can sit around waiting for life to happen,
or you can seize this very moment and
make things happen.

OCTOBER

8

When life seems overwhelming,
take a step back and keep it simple. Do one
thing at a time and do it the best you can.

You have the right to choose your own path.
Remember every day that the world is
full of opportunity to make your life
what you want it to be.

Tomorrow will take care of itself
if you take care of today.

'Be vigilant; guard your mind
against negative thoughts.'

Buddha

We are never given more than we can handle,
so hold tight to the belief that you can get
through anything – because you can!

This is my birthday, so I wanted to give you a really positive thought for
today. It's totally true that we have the ability to get through anything –
we just have to have confidence in ourselves. Keep going, ask for help
if you need to, and never give up! As I've said before –
if you believe, you will survive!

If you don't have the best of everything,
make the best of everything you have.

No matter how far away or how close
your goal, the only way you will reach it
is to take the next step towards it.

'Courage is the price that Life exacts
for granting peace.'
Amelia Earhart

Rock bottom is not a real place.
It's nothing but a feeling, and you can lift
yourself out of it if you choose.

OCTOBER

17

The difficult times teach us to appreciate
the good times. We would not know
happiness without sadness.

OCTOBER

18

Secrets will stifle you, so speak up
and share your worries with the people you
trust. A problem shared is a problem halved.

'I'm not afraid of storms,
for I'm learning to sail my ship.'
Louisa May Alcott

This is your only life,
so make it amazing!

OCTOBER

21

When you look at yourself, see a good friend
with whom you share the memories that
made you who you are today.

OCTOBER

22

Sometimes it's difficult to get started
because we don't know where to start.
Instead of looking for the start line, just begin
from exactly where you are now;
you'll soon be on your way.

OCTOBER
23

There are no deadlines for healing yourself;
keep looking forward and appreciate each
and every milestone along the way.

OCTOBER

24

'I'll walk where my own nature would be leading: It vexes me to choose another guide.'

Emily Brontë

OCTOBER

25

If you feel bored, help others.
If you feel helpless, help others. If you feel
lonely, unloved, lost or frail, help others who
need help most. Nothing will help you find
yourself more than helping others.

OCTOBER

26

We see what we choose to see;
life appears rich if you seek out its treasures.

You'll only know with hindsight if a decision was right or wrong, so, if you can't decide on something, take the risk and do it anyway. Follow your heart and you may find it was the right choice.

OCTOBER

28

If you want to fly,
just spread your wings.

'When one door closes another opens but we often look so long and so regretfully upon the closed door that we do not see the one which has opened for us.'
Alexander Graham Bell

OCTOBER

30

You will never know what you can do
until you do it. Step out of your comfort zone
and into the unexpected – what you achieve
will amaze you!

A crisis can be a positive thing –
it can encourage you to look at your life
and make choices about how you wish
to make it better.

NOVEMBER

NOVEMBER

1

Monthly Mantra

'I will focus on what I do have in life, rather than what I don't. I have wonderful people and good things in my life – I will remember to show my gratitude and never take them for granted.'

Even when it's cold and dark outside, we can find so many things to be thankful for – like warm fires, hot chocolate and other cosy comforts! You can apply the same way of thinking to your life. This mantra reminds you to focus on the good things in life and to count your blessings, helping you to stay positive even when you're feeling challenged.

2

Once you learn to love yourself,
you can begin to make the world
a more loving place.

Just because you've never done something,

it doesn't mean you can't.

'That it will never come again
is what makes life so sweet.'
Emily Dickinson

NOVEMBER
5

How much you achieve depends
on how much you believe in yourself.

When you decide to do something,
get on and do it. The sooner you do,
the more you'll achieve.

You cannot control what happens
around you, but you can control
what happens inside you.

'A wise man will make more
opportunities than he finds.'

Francis Bacon

NOVEMBER

9

Learn to love the darkness, it's the only time
you can truly see the stars.

I really love this saying. Someone said it to me when I was at rock
bottom and it suddenly made me see that even though I felt the worst
I'd ever felt in my life, there was still hope if only I could make the effort
to look for it. So when things feel really dark — open your eyes,
look up, and you might just begin to see the way out.

NOVEMBER
10

Our lives may be a labyrinth, but there is
always a way through.

Remember that great love and
great achievements involve great risk.
These are the risks in life worth taking.

A life full of meaning is more satisfying
than a life full of success.

When you look in the mirror,
see both the person you are now and the
person you want to be.

'I have dreamed in my life, dreams
that have stayed with me ever after,
and changed my ideas; they have gone
through and through me, like wine through
water, and altered the colour of my mind.'

Emily Brontë

You can choose which memories become
important to you: cherish the good ones
and learn from the bad.

Honesty invites honesty. Relationships
that are based on truth will lighten your soul
and be worthy of your love.

Make today all about having the day
you deserve. Decide it will be so, decide
to be kind to yourself, and then you
can make it happen.

NOVEMBER
18

'No matter how hard the past,
you can always begin again.'
Buddha

You can be as happy
as you allow yourself to be.

Put as much care into the small things
you do as into the big things in life,
and you will learn to appreciate everything
and everyone around you.

A tragedy can be the making of you.
With a positive spirit, you can create the best
times from the worst times and the pain
in your heart will heal.

NOVEMBER
22

The past is not for regretting. The emotions
you felt then and the actions you took are as
important as the ones you feel and take now;
they made you the person who you are today
and have given you wisdom for making
better decisions in the future.

Your beauty lies in your heart.
From there it can only grow.

'Nothing happens to us that we are
not fitted by nature to bear.'
Marcus Aurelius

It is when you begin to nurture your
hopes and dreams that you begin to grow
into the person you want to be.

NOVEMBER

26

It's easy to follow in another's footprints,
but it's much more fun to make your own.

Take the time to get to know and celebrate
who you are and everything you value
and believe in. Let these be your guides
in the journey of your life.

To risk nothing is worse than taking a risk;
when you risk nothing, there is no chance
you will win.

'You cannot find peace by avoiding life.'

Virginia Woolf

NOVEMBER
30

Have faith in yourself
and you can overcome anything.

DECEMBER

DECEMBER

1

Monthly Mantra

'I have achieved many things this year,
however small. I worked hard towards my
goals and will continue to do so. I am proud
of myself for doing my best!'

As the end of the year approaches, it's exciting to look back and see how
far you've come with all your goals and positive thinking. Repeat this
mantra and congratulate yourself on all your amazing progress!

The best friends are the ones
who love you just as you are,
whatever your situation.

'The tragedy of life is not that it ends so soon,
but that we wait so long to begin it.'

W. M. Lewis

When you remember to focus on other
people's good qualities, you will be reminded
that there is good in everyone.

DECEMBER

5

You are unique,
so dare to be yourself!

DECEMBER

6

The more effort you put into all
that you do, the more reward you will feel,
whatever the outcome.

'I try to avoid looking forward or backward,
and try to keep looking upward.'

Charlotte Brontë

If others believe in you, listen to them.
After all, they may be right!

All the world's a stage: choose the role
you want to play, and play it well!

Reinforce the actions that do you good and stop those that do you harm – on the inside or outside – before they become habit.

True courage is not the absence of fear,
it is taking action in spite of fear.

'Do not be embarrassed by your mistakes.
Nothing can teach us better than our
understanding of them.'
Thomas Carlyle

When things feel out of control, recall
moments when you felt safe – today you can
live them and breathe them again, and cherish
the peaceful spirit these memories bring.

Life is unpredictable; that is what makes it
so rich. Embrace all of life's surprises!

Shine your positive energy and self-belief on others and it will be reflected back at you.

The past is full of unanswered questions; let them go and embrace the unknown future.

Remind yourself every day that you matter.
Everyone has a contribution to make to the
world – no matter how big or small.

'The mind is everything;
what you think, you become.'
Buddha

Be the best you know you can be,
not the best that other people think
you should be.

The smallest things in life
can have the biggest impact, so never
underestimate their value.

DECEMBER

21

There is fulfilment to be found
all along the journey towards your dreams,
not just in the achievement. Take the time
to enjoy every step.

'The consciousness of loving and being loved
brings a warmth and richness to life
that nothing else can bring.'
Oscar Wilde

The things that bring the greatest joy
are the things that come for free.

This is a good time of year to take stock of all the positive things in our
lives that we normally take for granted. Instead of getting caught up
wishing for material things, or worrying that everyone else is having
a better time than you, just stop for a moment and think about all the
things you have going for you, such as the people who love you,
your health, your abilities and the little things in life
that make you smile.

DECEMBER

24

Remind yourself of how far you've come
in your journey; what you calmly do today
you may have feared to attempt
last week, month or year.

Receiving brings fleeting happiness,
but giving makes the feeling last.

Time spent with those you love

is time never wasted.

We are all capable of extraordinary things;
the spirit is within us to march forward
even when the road seems difficult.

Praise yourself generously and love
the way it feels. The only opinion about you
that really counts is yours.

'Life can only be understood backwards . . .
But it must be lived forwards.'

Søren Kierkegaard

When fear holds you in its grip,
fighting against it will only tighten its clutch.
When you say to yourself and trust that
all will be well, you'll feel it let you go.

DECEMBER

31

We cannot know the future,
we can only know the present.
Live today for all it can be.

ACKNOWLEDGEMENTS

Thank you to my dear family for always ensuring our home was a happy one full of love and positivity. Mum and Dad, thank you for tirelessly carrying out my physiotherapy sessions with *The Secret* always playing in the background. Even when we were not feeling so positive – it really did work.

Paul and Suzy, my darling brother and sister, even though we were all in the same house you still put pen to paper to write me such important letters with those precious words of encouragement, support and positivity – I still read them, even now.

Thank you to my beautiful friends Kay, Sammy, Lisa, Daisy, Nicky, Rita, Samuel, Kamran, Sofia and Donatella, who introduced me to affirmations books and who sent me beautiful notelets, postcards and letters – they are among some of my most treasured possessions.

To the two people who first put me on the right spiritual path and made me understand my life – Mr Jawad and Alice – thank you for your guidance, wisdom and positivity, you taught me so much. Thank you also Lucinda for explaining to me why, how and when to be quiet – I will meditate one day (when I get the time)!

A huge thank you to Jenny Heller, Ione Walder, Helena Caldon and all the teams at Quercus for the hard work, belief and love that went into this book. The positive vibes and affirmations that came from the Quercus building made this book happen!